PEOPLE AT WORK

Christopher McHugh

Wayland

Discovering art

Animals
Faces
Food
People at Work
Town and Country
Water

Cover Detail from *The Market in Tenochtitlán*, a mural by Diego Rivera in Mexico City.

Editor: Rosemary Ashley
Designer: David Armitage

First published in 1993 by
Wayland (Publishers) Limited
61 Western Road, Hove
East Sussex BN3 1JD
England

British Library Cataloguing in Publication Data
McHugh, Christopher
    People at Work. – (Discovering Art Series)
    I. Title.   II. Series
    704.9

    ISBN 0–7502–0400–1

Typeset by Type Study, Scarborough, England
Printed in Italy by G. Canale & C.S.p.A., Turin

Contents

1 Showing work in art

1 *An Ancient Egyptian carving in wood, showing farmers with oxen pulling a plough. British Museum, London.*

Work describes the things that most people do for much of their lives. It can be farmwork, factory work, housework; work indoors or outside; it can be interesting, boring, tiring or fun. Because work is such an important part of most people's lives, it has always been a popular subject for artists.

People work to grow and gather food, to build houses and towns, to make useful things and sometimes just to make money. Other activities can be called work too, as we will see later. Do you do any work? Look through this book and see if the pictures in it give you any ideas about the kinds of work you might like to try yourself.

The sculpture shown in picture **1** is from Egypt. It was made about 4,000 years ago and it shows how people have often used animals to help them with their work. Here, cattle pull a plough to prepare a field for planting crops.

Picture **2** is by the French painter Edgar Degas and shows a group of men working at the Cotton Exchange in New Orleans. They are looking at samples of cotton which have been gathered from cotton plants, and are agreeing prices for buying and selling the raw cotton. It is then spun into thread to be woven into cloth. On page 12 you can see the spinning and weaving processes of silk thread (pictures **12** and **13**).

2 The Cotton Exchange *by Edgar Degas. Musée des Beaux Arts, Paris.*

2 Work in ancient times

Of course people have always had to work just in order to live; from picking berries for food to operating a computer. Even in the most ancient art people are shown doing jobs. Picture **3** is a painting on the walls of a cave in Spain. It shows people with spears, bows and arrows. They may be hunting animals for food or fighting their enemies, but whatever they are doing is helping them to stay alive. The cave painting is believed to be about 10,000 years old.

Picture **4** shows a painting from the wall of a tomb in Ancient Egypt. Like picture **1**, it is also about 4,000 years old. Here two men are shown killing an enormous ox,

3 (below) *A very ancient painting on a cave wall at Valtorta in Spain.*

4 (opposite) *A painting on the wall of a tomb in Ancient Egypt, showing men slaughtering an ox. Egyptian Museum, Tunis.*

5 Building Sennacherib's Palace. *A relief carving in the British Museum, London.*

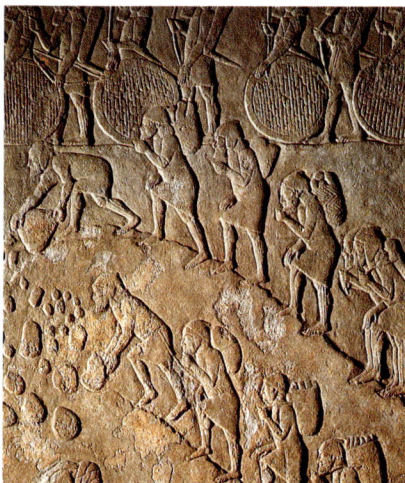

either for food or as a sacrifice to a god. Killing the animal seems to have been a tricky job, needing two people to tie up the feet and turn the animal over ready to have its throat cut. Can you see how the artist has shown the streams of red blood pouring down on to the floor?

Assyria was in a part of the world now usually called the Middle East, which used to be known as Mesopotamia. The Assyrians were warlike people who often used the people they conquered as slaves. Picture **5** is a relief that was carved on the wall of a palace at Nineveh, one of the greatest Assyrian cities. The relief shows slaves building the palace and it was made by carefully cutting away the front of a slab of stone to leave the picture standing out from the background.

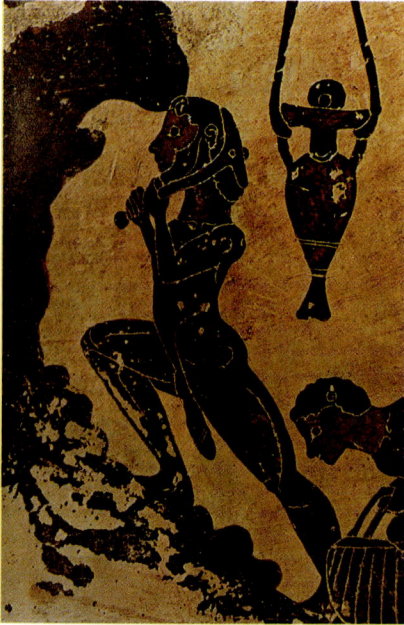

The Ancient Greeks lived in the islands and coastlands of the Aegean Sea, in the eastern Mediterranean. They developed a civilization and a style of art that was different from those of the other peoples around them. In picture **6** we see a painting of mine workers digging ore from the ground. It was painted on a wall about 2,500 years ago, at a time when the Greeks were using metals for tools and weapons. Like the builders in picture **5**, these workers are probably slaves too, captured by the Greeks in war.

6 (above) *A painting on a wall at Corinth in Greece, showing mine workers digging out ore from under ground.*

7 (right) *A decorated vase showing people harvesting olives. The British Museum, London.*

Picture **7** shows a Greek vase decorated with patterns and pictures. We can see workers gathering olives from the trees. Olives were an important crop for the Greeks and other peoples who lived around the Mediterranean Sea. Often the oil pressed from the olives would be used, like money, for buying and selling other goods.

Picture **8** is a Roman stone relief, made in a similar way to the one in picture **5**, but cut deeper (though now, as you can see, it is rather worn down). The Romans came from the city of Rome in Italy and, being very good soldiers and organizers, they swept across the Greek-owned lands and much of Europe, North Africa and the Middle East, creating an enormous empire. The relief shows a workshop where tools and weapons were made from metals such as iron and bronze.

8 *A relief sculpture showing two men in a workshop. Museum of Civilization, Rome.*

3 Work around the world

All around the world different types of work have helped people to live or to improve their lives. The picture on the cover of this book is by an artist from Mexico called Diego Rivera. Although he painted this picture in the twentieth century, he shows the ancient Mexican people called Aztecs. He has painted them making objects from clay, feathers and metal. Can you see the fire in which they are melting metal to pour into moulds?

There were many people living in the Americas before the arrival of Europeans (around the beginning of the 1500s). The Incas ruled a part of South America, in the area now called Peru. Picture **9** is a wooden vase made by an Inca artist, showing a woman looking after llamas. She is holding a bolas, a special rope weighted with heavy balls at each end, which, when thrown, wraps around the legs of an animal and makes it fall over. The vase was made about 800 years ago.

10 (opposite, top) *Part of a painted robe showing a buffalo hunt. Buffalo Bill Historical Center, Cody, Wyoming.*

11 (opposite, lower) *A bronze plaque of a drummer, from Benin in Nigeria. British Museum, London.*

9 *A ceremonial painted wooden vase. University Museum, Cuzco.*

Picture **10** shows part of a painted robe, made of buffalo hide (or skin), which was worn by a member of the Shoshoni tribe from the central plains of North America. The pictures painted on the hide show a buffalo hunt. These animals were important to many of the North American Indians for food, clothing and housing (hides were used to make shelters called tepees).

Picture **11** shows a very different type of work. This bronze plaque, made by an artist from Benin in West Africa, shows a man drumming for people to listen or dance to. The bronze plaque was made by melting the bronze in a very hot fire, pouring it into a mould and allowing it to cool and set hard. You can see this process being carried out in the cover picture.

Many inventions have come from China, one of the oldest civilizations in the world. Here we can see pictures of two stages of a very complicated work to produce silk cloth.

Picture **12** shows part of a beautifully decorated plate. The decoration shows the process of spinning silk thread from the cocoons of silkworms. The cocoons are coats which the little worms make to protect themselves while they turn into moths (just like caterpillars turn into butterflies). Having discovered what a very useful substance these cocoons formed, the Chinese invented ways of turning the silk into long threads, as they are doing in the picture.

12 (opposite, top) *Part of a beautifully decorated Chinese bowl.*

13 (opposite, lower) Weaving silk, *an eighteenth-century painting in the Victoria and Albert Museum, London.*

14 Carpenter's Yard *from* The Thirty-Six Views of Mount Fuji, *by Katsushika Hokusai. British Museum, London.*

Picture **13** is a painting made in China in the eighteenth century. It shows the silk threads being woven into cloth. This weaving process is similar to the process that is used to make the fluffy cotton shown in picture **2** into cotton cloth.

Picture **14** is a wood-block print by a famous Japanese artist called Katsushika Hokusai. He made many prints showing scenes of the countryside near Mount Fuji. Hokusai made his prints by cutting pictures into wooden blocks which were then covered in different coloured inks and pressed on to paper. This print shows a busy carpenter's yard where wood is prepared and stored ready for use. Notice the enormous stacks and piles of planks, strips and blocks. One man is throwing down blocks for another to catch. Another is cutting a huge chunk of wood into thinner pieces. Can you see the peak of Mount Fuji in the background?

15 *An Arabian manuscript painting showing a pharmacist mixing up medicines. Baghdad Museum, Iran.*

16 *Workmen building a palace, a painting from seventeenth-century India.*

Some jobs, like building, need strong arms and legs to lift and carry heavy weights. Others, like playing a musical instrument, need a lot of skill. Yet more jobs need a great deal of knowledge and care if they are to be done properly. Picture **15** shows this last kind of job. A pharmacist is someone who makes up medicines. Here we see an Arabian pharmacist making up a mixture in a pan, heating it over a fire. The picture is from a book illustrated long ago by an artist in the country we now call Iraq. Arabian people have introduced many sciences which are practised today all over the world, including mathematics and astronomy, as well as early ideas about medicine.

Picture **16** is from India. It was painted in the 1600s, when people from Persia (now called Iran) ruled much of India. Like picture **15**, it is made by an artist who belonged to the religion of Islam. This period of Indian art is called Mogul. In the picture many people are working to build a palace; how many different jobs can you count? Compare this picture to picture **5** on page 7, which shows Assyrian slaves building a palace. Although they are of very similar subjects, what would you say are the biggest differences between the two pictures?

Picture **17** is another painting from a book. This one was made in Germany in the 1500s. In this painting a group of village women are doing the laundry. They are heating water and washing and drying sheets and clothes. How has this sort of work changed and how would you show, in a picture, people doing laundry work today?

17 *A manuscript painting from Germany showing women laundering clothes. The British Library, London.*

4 Work in European art

From about 1400, people in Europe became especially interested in the art of the Ancient Greeks and Romans. Their amazing skills in showing how things looked were rediscovered and changed the way all European artists made pictures. This period, which began in Italy and lasted about two hundred years, is known as the Renaissance.

We can see how, a few years after the Renaissance, the Dutch painter, Jan Vermeer, liked to paint the appearances of ordinary things such as events going on inside a house. Because he made few paintings they have become

19 (opposite) A School for Boys and Girls, *by Jan Steen, National Gallery of Scotland.*

18 The Lacemaker, *by Jan Vermeer. Louvre, Paris.*

very precious and most are now in famous galleries and museums. In *The Lacemaker* (picture **18**) he shows us a woman intent on her work. Look how he has painted the light catching the wooden post that holds up the work bench and the patterned rug on the edge of the table.

Picture **19** is by Jan Steen, another Dutch artist working at about the same time. He shows us people doing completely different work. What sort of work does his painting show? The two schoolteachers certainly should be working, but are they? How many children can you spot who are really doing any school work?

Picture **20** is a painting by Georges de la Tour, a French artist painting at the same time as Vermeer and Steen. He has painted Jesus Christ as a child, helping his father Joseph in his carpenter's workshop. Like Vermeer, de la Tour is fascinated by light. What is the difference between the light shown in this picture and in *The Lacemaker*, picture **18**?

20 Christ with Saint Joseph, in the Carpenter's Shop *by Georges de la Tour. Louvre, Paris.*

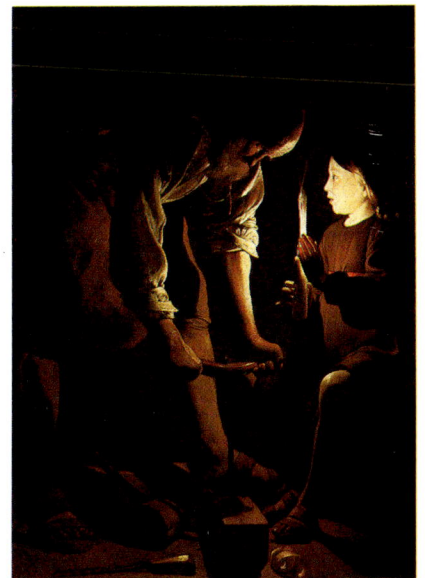

17

These next two paintings show very different types of work. Picture **21**, by the French artist Jean-Baptiste Chardin, is a little like Vermeer's painting (picture **18**, page 16). It also shows a woman working indoors. Chardin, like Vermeer, seems to enjoy showing the texture of objects and the light as it falls on them. Can you see the light shining on the washtub and the copper pan?

Picture **22**, by the Spanish painter Francisco de Goya, shows an outdoor scene of farming work, although nearly everybody in the picture has stopped to rest! If you turn back to the Egyptian sculpture, picture **1** on page 4, you can see how people long ago made art to show farm work. Goya's harvest picture gives us an idea of how such jobs may have been done in the 1700s.

22 Summer, or The Harvest, *by Francisco de Goya. Prado, Madrid.*

Picture **23**, by Philip de Loutherbourg, shows the changes that even in the 1700s were beginning to alter the way people worked. This was the start of the Industrial Revolution, which led to the first factories being built. Machines were being used to make many more products, faster than ever before. This revolution in the making of things (manufacturing) was to change work and life completely for most people, especially in Europe and America. It is often said that the Industrial Revolution began in England and de Loutherbourg's painting shows the early iron foundries at Coalbrookdale in Shropshire. He chose to make it a night scene, when the red glow of the furnaces lit up the smoky sky very dramatically.

23 Coalbrookdale at Night, *by Philip de Loutherbourg. Science Museum, London.*

24 The Wood Sawyers, *by Jean François Millet. Victoria and Albert Museum, London.*

In France, in the 1800s, some painters began to take a special interest in the older types of work. They liked to paint men and women carrying out the traditional tasks that people had been doing for centuries. This was partly because so many people were beginning to move to towns, to work in the factories, leaving the old styles of life behind.

One of these artists, Jean François Millet, wanted to show that those who worked on the land and in the farms were special people who somehow understood life better than those crowding the city streets. In picture 24 Millet shows two men using a large two-handled saw to cut a massive log into sections. Can you see the third woodcutter in the background? By painting a picture of these workers, Millet is showing us that they are worth special attention.

Gustave Courbet was another French artist, working at the same time as Millet. He also wanted to make different kinds of pictures from the usual choice of successful artists, who mostly painted portraits of famous and important people or pictures about religious or historical stories.

In picture **25** Courbet shows people working at a very ordinary job. Two men are breaking big stones into smaller ones to be used for building or road-making, and carrying them away in baskets. Can you see how the artist has shown the torn working clothes of the two stone breakers, and the effect of the hot sun as it beats down on them? Look at the shadow on the kneeling stone breaker's face cast by his hat.

25 The Stone Breakers, *by Gustave Courbet, Staatliche Kunstsammlungen, Dresden.*

Here are two paintings of carpenters at work. A carpenter is someone who works with wood, although those doing special carpentry jobs have other names, such as joiner or cabinet maker.

Gustave Caillebotte was an artist working in France just over a hundred years ago. He must have looked carefully at some carpenters working on a wooden floor before he set about painting this picture (picture **26**). He has painted the men working in a very realistic and lively way. What job is each man doing? Caillebotte seems to have shared some of his ideas about people at work with Courbet (see picture **25**, page 21). Look how he has painted the light reflected off the bare backs of the workmen and off the floor itself. Can you think of another picture in this book which also shows daylight falling from a window on to objects in a room?

26 Les Raboteurs du Parquet (Planing Parquet), *by Gustave Caillebotte. Musée d'Orsay, Paris.*

The English artist John Everett Millais was working in England at the same time as Caillebotte was working in France. Millais' painting (picture **27**) is very different to Caillebotte's painting (opposite). Millais liked to use his imagination a lot when he was making his pictures. He belonged to a group of English artists called the Pre-Raphaelites, who often made pictures about poems and stories. Millais' painting shows a story from the New Testament of the Bible. Jesus is shown as a little red-haired boy, with his parents and others, in his father's carpentry workshop in Nazareth. Can you see the sheep outside, through the open door?

Later in his life Millais became a rich and successful artist, painting mostly portraits. Compare this picture of Jesus in the carpenter's workshop with the one painted by Georges de la Tour, picture **20** on page 17. What do you think are the biggest differences between the two paintings?

27 Christ in the House of His Parents, *by John Everett Millais. Tate Gallery, London.*

6 Work in modern art

The two pictures on these pages were both made in the 1800s, one was made in France and the other in the United States. Each shows that the artists were interested in painting pictures of real people doing real work, just as in pictures **24**, **25** and **26**.

We have already seen earlier works of art showing jobs like the ones shown on this page. We have seen a plaque with an African musician playing the drums and a picture from an Arabian book of a pharmacist making up medicine; (pictures **11** and **15** on pages 11 and 14).

28 Les Musiciens de l'Orchestre, *by Edgar Degas. Louvre, Paris.*

29 The Gross Clinic, *by Thomas Eakins. Jefferson College, Philadelphia.*

In picture **28** Edgar Degas shows us the hard work that goes into making an evening's entertainment. He painted only part of the dancers lit up on stage and nothing of the audience enjoying themselves. Instead he wanted us to look particularly at the members of the orchestra, who are working hard to provide the music for the dancers, from the dark area below and in front of the stage.

The anatomy lesson (picture **29**) showing all the gory details of an operation on a dead body, was painted by American artist Thomas Eakins. How many hands can you see with blood on them? The doctor in charge is doing two important jobs. He is finding out how the human body works and passing on the information to his students.

30 The Builders, *by Fernand Léger. Musée Léger, Biot.* © *DACS, 1993.*

Moving into the twentieth century, we see how the full effects of the Industrial Revolution, which began in the 1700s (see picture **23**, page 19), have spread around the world. Cities have grown enormously; factories and machinery have changed completely, and many new types of work have been introduced. Artists, of course, have tried to show some of these changes in their works of art.

Picture **30** is a painting by the French artist Fernand Léger. It shows a number of workmen constructing a framework of iron girders for a large building – perhaps a skyscraper – using ladders and cranes. He has painted the picture in a very simple way. It looks almost like a cartoon, with bright colours and strong black outlines. The blue of the background is the sky, to show that the building is very tall.

Picture **31** is by Stanley Spencer, an English artist who mostly liked to paint pictures that were based on Bible stories. But during the Second World War (1939–45) he, along with other artists, was asked by the British Government to make pictures about what was happening at the time. Some of these artists painted battle scenes; others made pictures showing how people lived in wartime. Spencer chose to paint some extremely large pictures of the men building ships on Clydeside in Scotland. This is part of one of these paintings. Can you see any similarities between this picture and pictures **6**, and **8** on pages 8 and 9?

31 Shipbuilding on the Clyde – Burners, *by Stanley Spencer. Courtesy of the Trustees of the Imperial War Museum, London.*

Who are the artists and where are their works?

Gustave Caillebotte (1848–94) French
He was a member of the group of artists who came to be known as the Impressionists. He was influenced by the work of the famous Impressionist artist Claude Monet, who was one of his friends. Many of his paintings are of Parisian life in the second half of the nineteenth century. His work can be seen in Paris and the USA. Picture **26**, page 22.

Jean-Baptiste Siméon Chardin (1699–1779) French
A painter mainly of still lifes (objects such as flowers, fruit etc) and 'genre' pictures (scenes of everyday life). His paintings, which were usually quite small, are noted for their accurate representation. His works can be seen in major collections all over the world, including the Louvre in Paris, and the National Gallery in London. Picture **21**, page 18.

Gustave Courbet (1819–77) French
He was a self-taught artist who liked to shock people and get himself reported in the newspapers. He gave the title 'Realism' to his work because he liked to paint what he saw around him as honestly as he could. He had to leave France for political reasons, and died in exile in Switzerland. His works can be seen in major collections around the world. Picture **25**, page 21.

Edgar Degas (1834–1917) French
He was a member of the Impressionist group of painters although he disliked the name and refused to use it. Degas was one of the first artists to use photography to help him make his paintings. You can see his works in galleries all over the world, especially in the Musée d'Orsay in Paris, and at the Victoria and Albert Museum, the Tate and Courtauld Galleries and the National Gallery in London. Also in Cambridge, Edinburgh, Glasgow and Liverpool. Pictures **2** and **28**, pages 5 and 24.

Thomas Eakins (1844–1916) American
He was born and lived in Philadelphia, where he painted mainly portraits. He studied anatomy at medical college and this was to help him as an artist because his work was noted for its realistic detail. His painting *The Gross Clinic* shocked a lot of people when it was painted because the scene of the operation was so realistic. His works can be seen mainly in museums and galleries in the USA. Picture **29**, page 24.

Francisco de Goya (1746–1828) Spanish
He became a successful court painter, painting many portraits of the royal family and other important people, but he often showed unfavourable sides of their characters. In 1808 the French invaded Spain and Goya worked on a series of famous prints called *The Disasters of War*, which showed the cruelty and horror of war. His work can be seen in major collections all over the world, especially in the Prado in Madrid, at the National and Courtauld Galleries in London, and the National Gallery and the Phillips Collection in Washington. Picture **22**, page 19.

Katsushika Hokusai (1760–1849) Japanese
A famous artist of the *Ukiyo-e* style of printing. His work can be seen at the Fitzwilliam Museum in Cambridge, the British Museum, the Victoria and Albert Museum, London, and in museums and galleries throughout the world. Picture **14**, page 13.

Fernand Léger (1881–1955) French
A painter who followed the ideas of the cubist painters Picasso and Braque. He is best known for his paintings made from machine-like shapes. Late in his life he designed some huge murals for the United Nations building in New York. His works can be seen at the Tate Gallery, London, the Musée d'Art Moderne, Paris, and the Musée Leger at Biot in southern France. Picture **30**, page 26.

Philip James de Loutherbourg (1740–1812) French
He was born in Alsace, the region between France and Germany. After training as a painter he moved to England where he designed theatre scenery as well as painting pictures. His work can be seen mainly in collections in England and France, including the Science Museum in London. Picture **23**, page 19.

John Everett Millais (1829–96) English
He was a member of the Pre-Raphaelite group of artists in Victorian England. In later life he achieved great success and became President of the Royal Academy. His works can be seen in collections in Liverpool, Manchester, Birmingham, Oxford, Cambridge and other cities in Britain. Also in London, at the Tate, National Portrait and Guildhall galleries. Picture **27**, page 23.

Jean François Millet (1814–75) French
He came from a poor farming family but trained as an artist with the famous painter Delaroche in Paris. He moved to a village outside Paris where he painted scenes of peasants labouring hard in the fields. His work can be seen in collections in France, Austria and the USA; and in Cardiff, Edinburgh, Glasgow and the National Gallery and Victoria and Albert Museum in London. Picture **24**, page 20.

Diego Rivera (1886–1957) Mexican
He worked in Paris in the early years of the twentieth century and knew many of the other artists working there at the time, such as Picasso and Braque. In 1921 he returned to Mexico, where many of his most famous works were huge murals, for which he borrowed ideas from ancient Mexican art. His works, especially the murals, can be seen mostly in Mexico, and in the USA. Cover picture.

Stanley Spencer (1891–1959) English
He is one of the most unusual English painters of the first half of the twentieth century. Many of his paintings are of religious subjects. He was greatly influenced by his experiences in the First World War (1914–18) and became a 'war artist' during the Second World War (1939–45), painting people working in the Scottish shipyards. You can see his works in the Spencer Gallery at Cookham, his home village on the Thames, and in collections in Aberdeen, Belfast, Cambridge, Birmingham, Hull, Leeds and London (at the Imperial War Museum and Tate Gallery). Also in Canada and the USA. Picture **31**, page 27.

Jan Steen (1626–79) Dutch
A painter mainly of everyday scenes, called genre pictures, which are also often funny. Like many of the Dutch artists of his time he had more than one job. At one time he ran a brewery and he also ran a tavern (or pub). He painted a large number of pictures, which can be seen in the National Gallery, London and in major collections all over the world. Picture **19**, page 17.

Georges de la Tour (1593–1652) French
He painted mostly religious subjects and he was fascinated by the effects of light, especially candle light at night. He learnt from the Dutch and Flemish artists of his time, who had themselves studied the extreme light and dark shadows in paintings by the Italian artist Caravaggio. Picture **20**, page 17.

Jan Vermeer (1632–1675) Dutch
Until early this century Vermeer's works were almost completely forgotten, but he is now considered to be one of the world's greatest painters. His paintings can be seen in major art collections around the world, including the Rijksmuseum and Mauritshuis in the Netherlands, and in the National Gallery and Kenwood House in London. Picture **18**, page 16.

Glossary

Anatomy The study of the structure of the body.

Astronomy The scientific study of the stars and planets.

Bronze A type of metal made from copper and tin, used for making tools and sculptures.

Cartoon An amusing, simplified drawing usually making fun of something or someone.

Civilization A stage in the development of the way people live together in groups.

Cocoon The silky cases that insects such as silkworms make around themselves before they turn into adults.

Cotton Exchange A place in New Orleans where raw cotton was bought and sold.

Foundries Workshops where iron is shaped by casting it in a mould.

Furnaces Very large ovens in which great heat is produced (for making steel, for instance).

Genre Describing a picture of people carrying out everyday activities.

Impressionists A group of artists painting towards the end of the nineteenth century in France. They recorded their impressions of light through the colours in their work.

Industrial Revolution The time during the eighteenth and nineteenth centuries when European countries and the USA changed from being mainly agricultural to mainly industrial nations.

Islam The religion of Muslims, who follow the teachings of the Prophet Muhammad.

Llamas Animals living in South America which are related to camels, but without any humps. They are bred for their wool and meat.

Mathematics The branch of knowledge to do with numbers, measurements and quantities, and how they relate to each other.

Mogul The period when people from Persia ruled India.

Moulds Shapes into which a melted liquid substance is poured. The substance takes on the shape of the mould as it hardens.

Ore Rock from which metals can be obtained.

Plaque An ornamental plate made from wood, porcelain or metal.

Pre-Raphaelites A group of artists in nineteenth-century England who made very detailed pictures, often of stories or poems, in a style they considered to be typical of early Renaissance artists.

Realistic Having a believable appearance.

Relief A picture which is raised, or partly three-dimensional.

Renaissance A time of rediscovery in Europe of the ideas from Ancient Greece and Rome

Sacrifice An offering to a god or gods.

Slaves People who are taken by force and made to work for others against their will.

Traditional According to custom.

Wood-block print A print using blocks of wood. The surface surrounding the design is cut away from the block to leave the design standing out from the background. Ink is put on to the block, which is pressed on to paper or cloth so the ink is transferred. A new block is needed for each different colour. Potato prints and lino prints are made in the same way.

Books to read

The Book of Art – A Way of Seeing (Ernest Benn, 1979)

Every Picture Tells a Story by Rolf Harris (Phaidon, 1989)

History of Art for Young People by A.F. and H.W. Janson (Thames and Hudson, 1989)

Just Look . . . A Book about Paintings by Robert Cumming (Viking Kestrel, 1979, reprint 1986).

Painting and Sculpture by Jillian Powell (Wayland, 1989)

The Penguin Dictionary of Art and Artists (Penguin, 1989)

People in Art by Anthea Peppin (Merlion Arts Library, 1992)

20th Century Art by Jillian Powell (Wayland, 1989)

Work – through the eyes of artists by Wendy and Jack Richardson (Macmillan, 1989)

Index

Picture acknowledgements

The publishers have attempted to contact all copyright holders of the illustrations in this title, and apologise if there have been any oversights.

The photographs in this book were supplied by: Bridgeman Art Library 16, 17(lower), 19(top), 22, 24, 25,/Giraudon 17, 24; ET Archives cover, 9, 10, 19(lower), 20 23; Michael Holford © 4, 7(lower), 12(lower); Imperial War Museum 27; Ronald Sheridan Library 6,8 (both), 12(top) 14(top); Wayland Picture Library/ Musée des Beaux Arts 5/British Museum 13/British Library 15, 17(top)/Art Studio Jaques Mer 26; Werner Foreman 7(top), 11(both), 14(lower). *The Builders* by Fernand Léger appears by kind permission of the copyright holders © DACS, London 1993, and *Shipbuilding on the Clyde* by Stanley Spencer © Imperial War Museum.